My First NFL Book

CLEVELAND BROWNS

Nate Cohn

LET'S READ
AV²
BY WEIGL™
ADDED VALUE • AUDIO VISUAL

Go to **www.av2books.com**, and enter this book's unique code.

BOOK CODE

Y472296

AV² by Weigl brings you media enhanced books that support active learning.

AV² provides enriched content that supplements and complements this book. Weigl's AV² books strive to create inspired learning and engage young minds in a total learning experience.

Your AV² Media Enhanced books come alive with...

 Audio
Listen to sections of the book read aloud.

 Video
Watch informative video clips.

 Embedded Weblinks
Gain additional information for research.

 Try This!
Complete activities and hands-on experiments.

 Key Words
Study vocabulary, and complete a matching word activity.

 Quizzes
Test your knowledge.

 Slide Show
View images and captions, and prepare a presentation.

... and much, much more!

Published by AV² by Weigl
350 5th Avenue, 59th Floor
New York, NY 10118

Website: www.av2books.com

Copyright ©2018 AV² by Weigl

Library of Congress Control Number: 2017930540

ISBN 978-1-4896-5496-0 (hardcover)
ISBN 978-1-4896-5498-4 (multi-user eBook)

Printed in the United States of America in Brainerd, Minnesota
1 2 3 4 5 6 7 8 9 0 21 20 19 18 17

032017
020317

Editor: Katie Gillespie
Art Director: Terry Paulhus

Weigl acknowledges Getty Images, Alamy, and iStock as the primary image suppliers for this title.

My First NFL Book

CLEVELAND BROWNS

CONTENTS

Team History

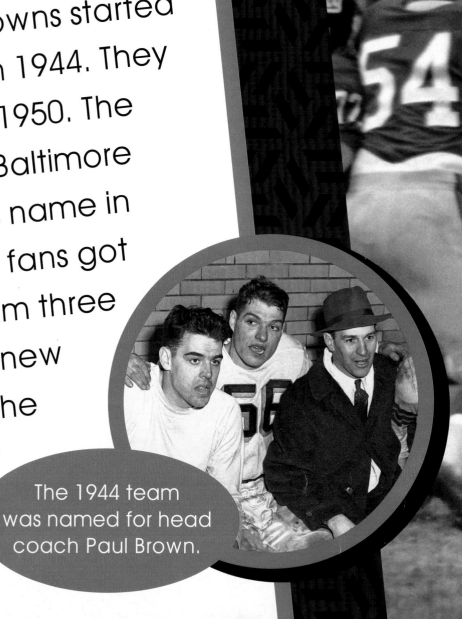

The Cleveland Browns started playing football in 1944. They joined the NFL in 1950. The team moved to Baltimore and changed its name in 1996. Cleveland fans got another NFL team three years later. The new team brought the Browns' name back to life.

The 1944 team was named for head coach Paul Brown.

5

The Stadium

The Browns play at FirstEnergy Stadium. It was built in 1998. There is a special area of bleacher seats in the east end zone. It is called the "Dawg Pound." Many of the fans who sit there dress up like dogs.

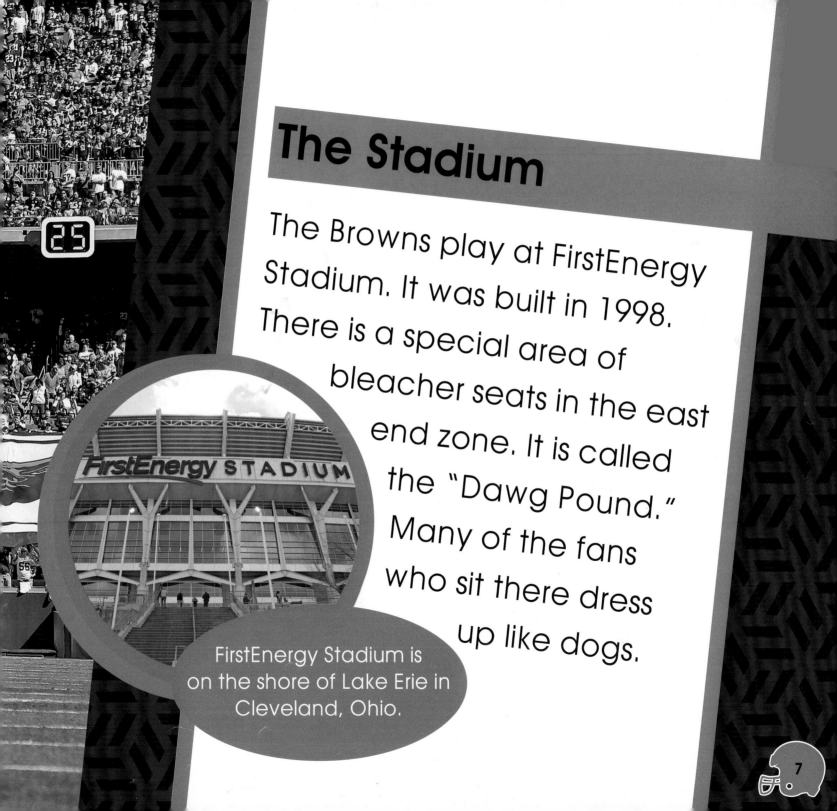

FirstEnergy Stadium is on the shore of Lake Erie in Cleveland, Ohio.

Team Spirit

The team mascot is a brown dog called Chomps. He leads cheers and does tricks. The team also has a real dog named Swagger. He leads the team onto the field and sits on the sidelines during games.

Swagger is a type of dog called a Bullmastiff.

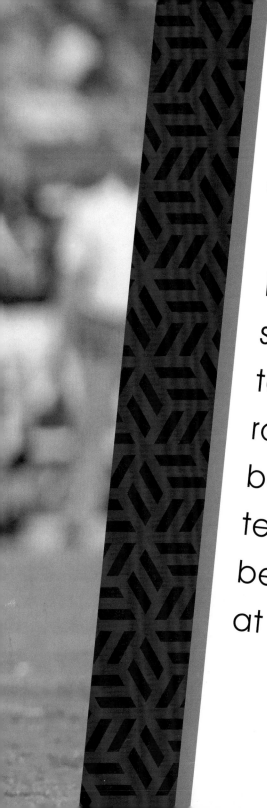

The Jerseys

The Browns' home jerseys are brown with white and orange stripes on the sleeves. The team wears white shirts on the road. The home jerseys have been brown for most of the team's history. The pants have been white, orange, or brown at different times.

The Helmet

The Browns' helmets are the only ones in the NFL without a drawing or logo on them. The helmets are solid orange with a brown and white stripe in the middle. The team does have a logo. It is a simple drawing of a helmet.

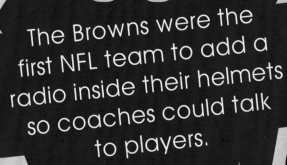

The Browns were the first NFL team to add a radio inside their helmets so coaches could talk to players.

The Coach

Hue Jackson became the Browns' head coach in 2016. Jackson is an expert at offense. He coached quarterbacks, wide receivers, and running backs before becoming a head coach. Jackson also coached special teams for college football. The special teams are the players who kick and punt.

Player Positions

The left tackle is usually the team's best pass blocker. This is because the left tackle protects the quarterback's blind spot. The blind spot for a right-handed quarterback is on the left side of the body. It is hard to see on that side when throwing.

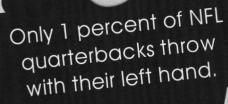

Only 1 percent of NFL quarterbacks throw with their left hand.

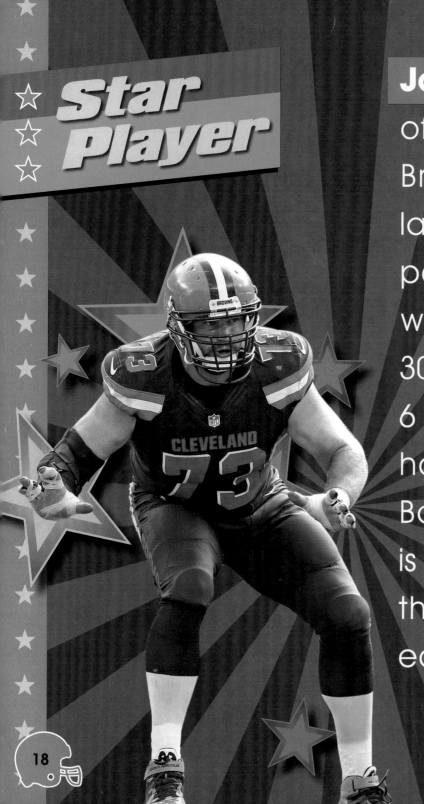

Star Player

Joe Thomas is an offensive tackle for the Browns. He is a very large and successful pass blocker. Thomas weighs more than 300 pounds and stands 6 feet, 6 inches tall. He has been to the Pro Bowl 10 times. That is the game played by the best NFL players each year.

Jim Brown is often called the best running back in history. He joined the Browns in 1957. Brown won Most Valuable Player awards from the press in four of nine seasons with the team. He had an average of 104.3 rushing yards per game. This is an NFL record.

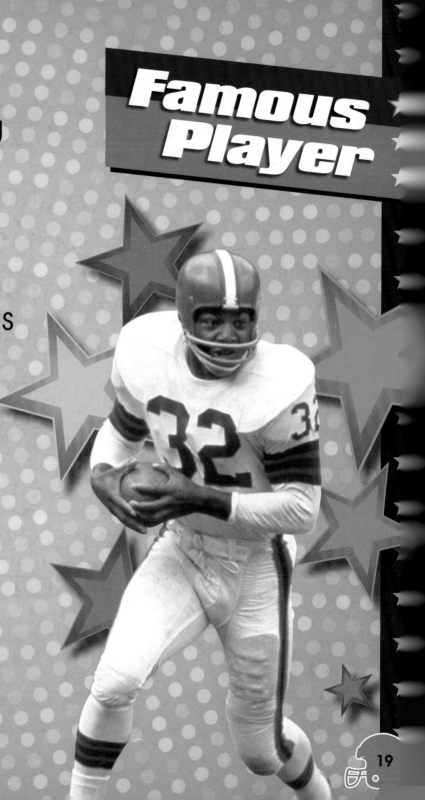

Team Records

The Browns have played in NFL playoff games 24 times since 1950. Receiver Terrelle Pryor used to be a quarterback. He had 1,000-yard seasons for both passing and receiving. This has been done by only one other NFL player. Steve Cox holds the team record for the longest field goal scored. It was 60 yards.

20

24 NFL Playoffs

Steve Cox

60-Yard Field Goal

Terrelle Pryor

1,000 Yards Passing and Receiving

21

By the Numbers

Quarterback Josh McCown holds the team record for most passing yards in **One game**. He threw **457** yards.

FirstEnergy Stadium seats

73,200

Browns fans.

Tight end Ozzie Newsome caught passes in **150 games** in a row.

Quarterback Otto Graham led the team to championship games **10 years in a row** from 1946 to 1955.

Joe Thomas is **one of only five** NFL players to play in the Pro Bowl in each of his first **10 seasons**.

Tackle and kicker Lou Groza was named **one of the greatest players** in the **first 75 years** of the NFL.

Quiz

1. Where is the "Dawg Pound" at FirstEnergy Stadium?

2. What is the name of the Browns' real team dog?

3. What did the Browns add inside their helmets?

4. How tall is Joe Thomas?

5. Which player had 1,000-yard seasons for both passing and receiving?

ANSWERS 1. East end zone 2. Swagger 3. A radio 4. 6 feet, 6 inches 5. Terrelle Pryor

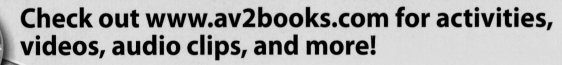

MEDIA ENHANCED BOOKS
AV² BY WEIGL™
ADDED VALUE • AUDIO VISUAL

The AV² Collection

Check out www.av2books.com for activities, videos, audio clips, and more!

1 Go to www.av2books.com.

2 Enter book code. **Y 4 7 2 2 9 6**

3 Fuel your imagination online!

www.av2books.com